# Salads Healthy Lunch

# Cookbook Vol.1

*This book contains low-fat, quick and easy recipes for beginners, ideated to boost your lifestyle from the awakening and balance your daily supply. Go through the Mediterranean diet to energize your mind and body healing!*

*Kumar Ortega*

# Table of Contents

# Welcome, dear reader!

This is my purpose to you.

This cookbook is a creation born from a researcher of the wellness. It's finalized to increase your energies and to let you live a happier life, without the heaviness of the modern kitchen.

In this book, you'll find my knowledge on how to keep your body and mind faculties active, productive and efficient.

Jump into a world of good habits and natural foods, if you want to discover the real deepness of your overall wellness.

Nevertheless, you'll learn new ideas, discover tastes of all around the world and change your meal plan in better.

Each of these dishes is thought to:

**1 - Let you wake up full of energies and keep this boost for all day long**

Thanks to light and natural greens as dinner and a high nutrient supply as brunch, you'll sleep better and be full of energies during the day.

**2 - Lose the excessive weight and keep your moral up**

As soon as you start to eat better and do physical activity, the leftover fat will disappear from your body and your image will finally become as you wish!

**3 - Improve your skills and surprise your friends**

Learn some new recipes taken from the worldwide tradition and twisted by a proper chef, only to let you discover modern tastes.

# Salad Recipes

# Superfood Bowl

Serves 4 pax

## Ingredients

- 2 Eggs
- 1/4 tsp Garlic powder
- 1 oz Kale
- 4 tsp Olive oil
- 1/4 tsp Paprika
- 10 oz Black beans
- 1 tbsp Black pepper
- 2 Chopped tomatoes
- 1/4 tsp Cumin
- 4 Tbsp Parmesan cheese
- 1 Sweet potato

## Procedure

1. Prepare your eggs in 4 teaspoons of oil. Next, toss in your kale until it begins wilting.

2. Add in low-sodium black beans, followed by the potatoes and tomatoes.

3. Toss on the seasonings and heat. Serve topped with parmesan cheese.

# Greens and Beans Salad

**Serves 6 pax**

## Ingredients

- 1 pound asparagus
- 1/2 red onion, sliced thin
- 15 ounces cannellini beans
- 6 ounces arugula
- Salt and pepper
- 3 tablespoons plus 2 teaspoons balsamic vinegar
- 5 tablespoons extra-virgin olive oil

## Procedure

1. Heat 2 tablespoons oil in 12-inch non-stick frying pan on high heat until just smoking. Put in onion and cook until lightly browned, about 1 minute.

2. Put in asparagus, 1/4 teaspoon salt, and 1/4 teaspoon pepper and cook, stirring intermittently, until asparagus is browned and crisp-tender, about 4 minutes.

3. Move to a container, mix in beans, and allow to cool slightly.

4. Beat vinegar, 1/4 teaspoon salt, and 1/8 teaspoon pepper together in a small-sized container. Whisking continuously, slowly drizzle in remaining 3 tablespoons oil.

5. Gently toss arugula with 2 tablespoons dressing until coated. Sprinkle with salt and pepper to taste.

6. Divide arugula among plates. Toss asparagus mixture with remaining dressing, arrange over arugula, and serve.

# Olives and Feta Salad

Serves 6 pax

## Ingredients

- 1/2 cup pitted kalamata olives
- 1 garlic clove
- 1/3 cup dill
- 1/3 cup pepperoncini
- 1 head escarole
- 3 tablespoons lemon juice
- 4 tablespoons extra-virgin olive oil
- Salt and pepper
- 4 ounces small head frisée
- 7 ounces feta cheese

## Procedure

1. Gently toss escarole, frisée, olives, feta, and pepperoncini together in a big container.
2. Beat dill, lemon juice, garlic, 1/4 teaspoon salt, and 1/8 teaspoon pepper together in a small-sized container.
3. Whisking continuously, slowly drizzle in oil. Sprinkle dressing over salad and gently toss to coat.
4. Serve.

# Vegs and Goat Cheese Salad

Serves 6 pax

## Ingredients

- 1 red bell pepper
- 1 shallot
- 1 garlic clove
- 1 pound asparagus
- 6 ounces spinach
- Salt and pepper
- 1 tablespoon plus 1 teaspoon sherry vinegar
- 6 ounces goat cheese
- 5 tablespoons extra-virgin olive oil

## Procedure

1. Heat 1 tablespoon oil in 12-inch non-stick frying pan on high heat until just smoking. Put in bell pepper and cook until lightly browned, approximately two minutes.
2. Put in asparagus, 1/4 teaspoon salt, and 1/8 teaspoon pepper and cook, stirring intermittently, until asparagus is browned and almost tender, approximately two minutes.
3. Mix in shallot and cook till they become tender and asparagus is crisp-tender, about 1 minute. Move to a container and allow to cool slightly.
4. Beat vinegar, garlic, 1/4 teaspoon salt, and 1/8 teaspoon pepper together in a small sized container.
5. Whisking continuously, slowly drizzle in remaining 1/4 cup oil. Gently toss spinach with 2 tablespoons dressing until coated. Sprinkle with salt and pepper to taste.
6. Divide spinach among plates. Toss asparagus mixture with remaining dressing and arrange over spinach. Sprinkle with goat cheese and serve.

# Beef Salad

**Serves 2 pax**

## Ingredients

- 1 Navel orange
- 0.5 oz Sweet piquante peppers
- 4 oz Grape tomatoes
- 2 Tbsp Fromage blanc
- 0.5 tsp Garlic powder
- 0.5 tsp Smoked paprika
- 1 tsp Chile powder
- 1 Sweet potato
- 8 oz Lean beef
- 1 Green or red leaf lettuce
- 1 tsp Olive oil
- 0.5 tsp Dried oregano
- 0.5 tsp Ground cumin
- 4 oz Mini sweet peppers

## Procedure

1. Whisk the paprika, chili powder, garlic powder, cumin, and oregano; set aside.
2. Spread the sweet peppers and potato on a large baking tray and drizzle them with 0.5 tsp. olive oil; top with half the spice mixture and toss to coat.
3. Bake at 450°F until browned and fork tender, 17 to 19 minutes. Remove from the oven.
4. While the vegetables are baking, combine the lettuce, tomatoes, piquante peppers, and orange.
5. Add the beef in a bowl and coat with remaining spice mixture.
6. Heat 0.5 tsp. olive oil in a medium nonstick skillet using the med-high temperature setting. Then add the beef in an even layer. Cook until lightly browned (2-3 min.).
7. Transfer the pan to a cool burner or the countertop and stir together the cilantro pesto and fromage blanc; add it to the lettuce mixture. Add the sweet potato and pepper mixture, then top with the beef and serve.

# Cucumber and Lemongrass Salad

Serves 8 pax

## Ingredients

- 1/4 cup minced mint
- 1/4 cup minced parsley
- 1/2 cup shredded carrot
- 1/2 cup white vinegar
- 1 cup bean sprouts
- 1 cup cubed tart apple
- 1 garlic clove, very thoroughly minced
- 1 tablespoon fish sauce
- 1 tablespoon vegetable oil
- 1 Thai chili, very thoroughly minced
- 2 stalks lemongrass
- 3 cups thinly cut cucumber

## Procedure

1. In a small deep cooking pan, mix the vinegar, chili, and garlic. Bring the mixture to its boiling point.
2. Cover the pan, take it off the heat, and allow to cool.
3. Trim and finely cut 1 lemongrass stalk. Put it in a small deep cooking pan with 1/2 cup of water, cover, and bring to its boiling point. Turn off heat and allow to cool.
4. Trim the rest of the lemongrass stalk, peel off the tough outer layers, and finely mince the white portion of the soft stalk within. Reserve roughly 1 tablespoon.
5. Mix the cucumber, bean sprouts, apple, carrot, mint, and parsley in a big mixing container.
6. In a small container mix the fish sauce, oil, minced lemongrass, the vinegar mixture, and the lemongrass water.
7. Toss the vegetables with the lemongrass vinaigrette to taste.

# Nicoise Salad

Serves 4 pax

## Ingredients

- 0.33 cups Light salad dressing
- 5 oz Arugula
- 2 cups Grape tomatoes
- 5 oz Tuna
- 0.25 cups olives
- 4 Hard-boiled eggs

## Procedure

1. Toss the salad greens with 3 Tbsp. of the Italian dressing. Place on serving plates.
2. Arrange the eggs, tomatoes, olives, and tuna on the lettuce.
3. Top with the remaining dressing and serve immediately.

# Balsamic Salad

Serves 4 pax

## Ingredients

- 3 cups Mixed salad greens
- 1 cup cherry tomatoes
- 1 Cucumber
- 0.25 cups balsamic vinaigrette

## Procedure

1. Toss each of the fixings into a large mixing container until the vegetables are evenly coated with dressing.
2. Put in a bowl and serve.

# Pear and Arugula Salad

**Serves 6 pax**

## Ingredients

- 2 Tbsp Balsamic vinegar
- 0.5 tsp Black pepper
- 2 Tbsp ex-virgin-Olive oil
- 0.5 oz Pecorino Romano cheese
- 1 Pear
- 6 oz Arugula
- 0.25 cups Walnut pieces

## Procedure

1. In a large salad bowl, top the arugula with the pear. Sprinkle the walnuts over the pear, then use a vegetable peeler to shave the cheese over the walnuts.
2. Drizzle the salad with the vinegar and oil.
3. Sprinkle it with the pepper and thoroughly toss.
4. Sprinkle with the Pecorino Romano cheese before serving.

# Veggie Noodle Salad

Serves 6 pax

## Ingredients

- 1 cup bean sprouts
- 1 lime
- 1/4 pound snow peas
- 1/2 cup toasted peanuts
- 1 medium carrot
- 4 green onions
- 8 ounces dried rice noodles
- 1 small red bell pepper
- 1 teaspoon sesame oil
- 1 teaspoon soy sauce
- 10 basil leaves, shredded
- 2 teaspoons vegetable oil

## Procedure

1. In a big container, toss the noodles with the oils and the soy sauce.
2. Blanch the snow peas in boiling water for half a minute and then wash them under cold water.
3. Put in the snow peas, bell pepper, and the carrot to the noodles and toss.
4. Sprinkle the basil, half of the green onions, and half of the bean sprouts, and toss thoroughly.
5. To serve, put the noodle salad on a chilled serving platter.
6. Spread the rest of the green onions, remaining bean sprouts, and the peanuts over the top.
7. Squeeze the juice of 2 lime wedges over the whole dish and use the rest of the wedges as decorate.
8. Serve instantly.

# Beefy Salad

Serves 4 pax

Ingredients

**For the dressing**

- 1/4 teaspoon black pepper
- 2 cloves garlic
- 1/4 cup basil leaves
- 2 tablespoons chopped serrano chilies
- 2 tablespoons fish sauce
- 1/4 cup lemon juice
- 2 tablespoons brown sugar

**For the salad**

- 1 small cucumber
- 1/2 cup mint leaves
- 1 pound beef steak

- 1 small red onion
- 1 tomato
- 5 Romaine lettuce leaves
- 1 stalk lemongrass

## Procedure

1. Mix all of the dressing Ingredients in a blender and pulse until well blended; set aside.
2. Flavor the steak with salt and pepper. Over a hot fire, grill to moderate-rare (or to your preference). Move the steak to a platter, cover using foil, and allow to rest for five to ten minutes before carving.
3. Cut the beef across the grain into thin slices.
4. Put the beef slices, any juices from the platter, and the rest of the salad Ingredients, apart from the lettuce, in a big mixing container.
5. Put in the dressing and toss to coat.
6. Serve placing lettuce leaves on separate plates and mound the beef mixture on top of the lettuce.

# Calamari Salad

Serves 4 pax

## Ingredients

### For the dressing

- 1 small onion
- 1 stalk lemongrass
- 1 red chili peppers
- 3 kaffir lime leaves
- 5 teaspoons lime juice
- 1 cup water

### For the salad

- 1 green onion, thinly cut
- 1 pound calamari, cleaned
- 6–8 sprigs cilantro
- 20 mint leaves, chopped

## Procedure

1. Mix all the dressing Ingredients in a small container; set aside.
2. Prepare a grill or broiler. Put the calamari on a broiler pan or in a grill basket and cook using high heat until soft, approximately 3 minutes per side.
3. Allow to cool to room temperature. Put the grilled calamari in a mixing container. Mix the dressing and pour it over the calamari.
4. If serving instantly, put in the mint, cilantro, and green onions.
5. To serve, use individual cups or bowls to help capture some of the wonderful dressing.

# Shrimp Noodle Salad

Serves 6 pax

## Ingredients

- 1 clove garlic
- 1 cup citrus fruit
- 1 teaspoon red pepper flakes
- 3/4 cup lime juice
- 1 medium tomato
- 1 stalk lemongrass
- 3 tablespoons fish sauce
- 24 medium shrimp
- 1 cup peanuts
- Salt and ground pepper
- 2 green onions
- 1 tablespoon brown sugar
- 1 tablespoon vegetable oil
- 8 ounces rice noodles

## Procedure

1. Soak the rice noodles in hot water for ten to twenty minutes and bring a pot of water to boil.
2. In the meantime, in a big container, combine the lemongrass, citrus, peanuts, tomato, scallions and cilantro.
3. In a small container, mix the red pepper flakes, garlic, sugar, lime juice, and fish sauce.
4. Drain the noodles from their soaking liquid and put in them to the boiling water.
5. When the water returns to its boiling point, drain them again and wash meticulously with cold water. Allow the noodles to drain well.
6. Put in the noodles and the dressing to the citrus mixture and toss to blend. Set aside.
7. Brush the shrimp with the vegetable oil and sprinkle with salt and pepper.
8. Grill or sauté for roughly two minutes per side or until done to your preference.
9. To serve, put the grilled shrimp on top of the noodles and decorate with peanuts.

# Spanish Salad

Serves 6 pax

## Ingredients

- 12 mushrooms
- 12 cherry tomatoes
- 1 head iceberg lettuce
- 3 carrots
- 1 cup green beans
- 4 ounces salami
- 12 spears white asparagus
- 1 cup green olives
- 4 ounces chorizo
- 1/2 onion
- extra virgin olive oil
- balsamic vinegar
- salt

## Procedure

1. Wash and chop the lettuce. Place in the center of a large platter.
2. Ring the rim of the platter with tomato halves.
3. Add onion rings in the center. Arrange asparagus like wheel spokes with tips radiating outwards from center.
4. Add carrots, mushrooms, green beans, salami and chorizo to the center. Sprinkle olives around platter edge.
5. Add salt and balsamic vinegar to taste. Drizzle well with olive oil.
6. Serve immediately.

# Spiced Rice Salad

Ingredients

**For the dressing**

- 1/4 cup sesame oil
- 1/2 cup fish sauce
- 1/4 cup hot chili oil
- 1/4 cup lime juice
- 1/2 cup rice vinegar

**For the salad**

- 1 sweet red pepper, seeded and diced
- 1 serrano chili pepper, seeded and minced
- 2 cups long-grained rice
- 2 carrots
- 1 cup chopped mint

- 1 cup chopped cilantro
- 8 lime wedges
- 6 green onions, trimmed and thinly cut
- 1 pound cooked shrimp
- 1 cup chopped unsalted peanuts

## Procedure

1. Whisk together all of the dressing Ingredients; set aside.
2. Cook the rice in accordance with the package directions. Fluff the rice, then move it to a big mixing container. Allow the rice to cool slightly.
3. Pour roughly of the dressing over the rice and fluff to coat. Continue to fluff the rice every so frequently until it is completely cooled.
4. Put in the green onions, carrots, red pepper, serrano chili pepper, mint, cilantro, and shrimp to the rice. Toss with the rest of the dressing to taste.
5. Place on separate plates and decorate with peanuts and lime wedges.

# Olive Oil on Garden Salad

Serves 4 pax

## Ingredients

- 1 cup alfalfa sprouts
- 5 cups mixed lettuce
- 1 cup radicchio 1 cup carrot
- 1 red onion
- 8 cherry tomatoes
- 24 slices cucumber
- 1 cup olive oil
- 1/4 cup balsamic vinegar
- 1 sprig fresh oregano
- 1 sprig fresh thyme
- Salt and pepper to taste

## Procedure

1. Mix lettuce, radicchio, alfalfa sprouts, carrots and onions in large bowl. Add cherry tomatoes and cucumber slices.
2. Combine the oregano, thyme, oil, vinegar, salt and pepper in a glass bowl.
3. Divide the garden salad evenly onto four serving plates. Drizzle dressing over the salads.

# Coconut Salad

Serves 6 pax

## Ingredients

- 1 recipe Coconut Marinade
- 1 cup jicama
- 1 medium cucumber
- 2 tablespoons basil

## Procedure

1. Put the jicama, cucumber, and basil in a big container.
2. Pour the marinade over the vegetables.
3. Allow to rest in your fridge for minimum 2 hours before you serve.

# Healthy Brunch

# Raspberry Smoothie Pops

Serves 4 pax

## Ingredients

- 1 cups raspberries
- 0.5 cups Skim milk
- 2 oz berry Greek yogurt
- 1 Banana

## Procedure

1. Measure and add each of the fixings in a blender. Puree the mixture until it's creamy smooth.
2. Pour the smoothies into four cups, ice-pop molds, or ice cube trays.
3. Insert sticks and pop them into the freezer upright until they freeze solid, about 3 hours.
4. Serve.

# Lemon Blueberry Yogurt Bars

Serves 16 pax

## Ingredients

- 2 squeezed lemon juice
- 1 tsp Maple syrup
- 0.75 cups Blueberries
- 1 Tbsp. plus 2 tsp Lemon zest
- 3 Tbsp Avocado oil
- 1.5 cups Unsweetened graham cracker flour
- 4 Eggs (1 large and 3 large egg whites)
- 2 cups vanilla Greek yogurt
- 0.25 tsp Salt

## Procedure

1. Lightly spray the parchment paper lined pan with a spritz of nonstick spray.

2. Toss these into the food processor: Graham cracker flour, avocado oil, 2 tsp. lemon zest, and salt; pulse to combine. Pat the mixture into the bottom of the parchment-lined pan.

3. Bake the crust at 350°F until golden brown (10-15 min.). Set the pan aside to cool but don't turn off the oven.

4. In a blender, puree the nonfat yogurt, egg, egg whites, maple syrup, and 1 Tbsp. lemon zest until smooth. Stir in the blueberries and pour onto the crust.

5. Bake until no longer jiggly in the center, 25-30 minutes. Place the pan on a wire rack to thoroughly cool.

6. Cut into 16 equal squares.

7. Serve.

# Breakfast Quiche

Serves 6 pax

## Ingredients

- 7 oz Green chiles
- 0.25 cups Skim milk
- 0.25 cups Whole wheat flour
- 3 eggs
- 0.5 cups Egg whites or egg substitute
- 1 cup Shredded cheddar cheese
- 1 cup Cottage cheese
- 0.5 tsp Baking powder

## Procedure

1. Beat the eggs using an electric mixer. Mix in the baking powder and flour until incorporated. Stir in egg whites and milk, mixing until smooth.
2. On low speed, mix in chiles, cottage cheese puree and shredded cheese.
3. Spread the batter in a 9" square or round baking dish coated with a spritz of cooking oil spray.
4. Bake at 400° Fahrenheit for 15 minutes. Adjust the temperature setting to 350° Fahrenheit and bake until the top is golden brown and the quiche is firm, about 25 more minutes. Cut in six pieces.
5. Serve immediately.

# Chocolate-Chia Breakfast Smoothie

**Serves 1 pax**

## Ingredients

- 0.5 tsp Cinnamon
- 1 banana
- 2 Tbsp Cocoa powder
- 2 oz Almond milk
- 2 Tbsp Chia seeds
- 2 Tbsp Peanut butter powder

## Procedure

1. In a bowl, mix together 1/2 c. almond milk with chia seeds and cinnamon and leave for at least 10 minutes, allowing the seeds to swell.
2. Take the banana, remaining almond milk, cocoa powder, and peanut butter powder, and combine in a blender until smooth.
3. Put chia pudding on the bottom of a large glass, then top with the smoothie.

# Banana Oat Peanut Butter

Serves 24 pax

## Ingredients

- 1 tsp Baking soda
- 2 Tbsp Brown sugar blend
- 2 cups oats
- 0.25 cups Ground flax seed
- 1 Banana
- 1 Egg
- 0.5 tsp Salt
- 1 tsp Vanilla extract
- 0.5 cups Peanut butter

## Procedure

1. Warm the oven at 350° Fahrenheit. Prepare a baking tray with a layer of parchment baking paper.
2. Mix the egg, banana, peanut butter, vanilla extract, and Splenda sugar blend in an over-sized mixing container.
3. Stir in the oats, baking soda, salt, and flaxseed in a small bowl until thoroughly mixed.
4. Stir the oat mixture into the peanut butter batter. Mix well.
5. Spoon batter into 1 Tbsp. balls and arrange them on the prepared pan.
6. Bake for 10 to 12 minutes, then place them on a wire rack to cool.
7. Serve.

# Crepes

Serves 4 pax

## Ingredients

- 1/2 cup water
- 1 cup all-purpose flour
- 2 eggs
- 1/2 cup milk
- 1/4 teaspoon salt
- 3 tablespoons butter, melted

## Procedure

1. Whisk eggs in large bowl.
2. Slowly add milk and water as you stir.
3. Stir until combined. Sift in flour.
4. Add salt and butter.
5. Beat until smooth.
6. Lightly oil frying pan.
7. Heat on medium high.
8. Pour 1/4 cup batter into pan and swish to coat.
9. Cook the crepe for 2 minutes.
10. When bottom is light brown, turn and cook other side.

# Summer Fruit Smoothie

Serves 4 pax

## Ingredients

- 6 oz Peach Greek yogurt
- 2 Peaches
- 1 cup Strawberries
- 0.5 cups Ice
- 1 cup Blueberries
- 1 Tbsp Ground flax seed
- 1 cup Almond milk

## Procedure

1. Toss each of the fixings into a blender, working the mixture until it's creamy smooth.
2. Serve chilled.

# Ricotta Cheese and Spinaches Crepes

Serves 8 pax

## Ingredients

- 1 tablespoon olive oil
- 1 onion
- 1 garlic clove, crushed
- 8 ounces spinach
- 1/4 cup pine nuts
- 1 cups tomato puree
- 1 cup coarsely grated cheddar
- Salt to taste
- 1 cup fresh ricotta cheese
- A pinch ground nutmeg
- 8 fresh made crepes
- Grounded black pepper to taste

## Procedure

1. Preheat oven to 350°F.

2. Wash spinach and trim ends. Chop onion fine.

3. Place spinach in large saucepan on medium heat. Cover and cook 3-4 minutes, stirring occasionally.

4. Drain well and set aside 5 minutes until cooled. Squeeze out moisture from spinach and chop coarsely. Place chopped spinach in large bowl.

5. Toast pine nuts 2 minutes in a medium sauté pan on high heat. Add toasted pine nuts to the spinach.

6. Add olive oil to sauté pan and heat on medium heat. Add onion and garlic and sauté5 minutes, stirring occasionally. Transfer onion and garlic to the bowl of spinach.

7. Add ricotta and nutmeg. Stir until well mixed.

8. Season crepe filling to taste with salt and pepper.

9.  Place crepe on clean work surface. Divide spinach filling into 8 equal portions. Spoon 1 portion of spinach filling into the center of the crepe. Roll up tight to enclose filling.
10. Place filled crepe in large baking dish.
11. Repeat with remainder of crepes and filling to form rows of crepes in the baking dish.
12. Spoon tomato puree over crepes. Sprinkle with cheddar cheese. Bake in oven for 20 minutes.
13. Crepes are done when cheese melts and crepes are heated throughout.

# Gluten-Free Parmesan Biscuit

Serves 12 pax

## Ingredients

- 3 Tbsp Trans-fat-free margarine
- 0.33 cups Skim milk
- 2 Tbsp Parmesan cheese
- 1 cup Gluten-free baking mix

## Procedure

1. Prepare a baking tray with a spritz of cooking oil spray.
2. Toss the baking mix and margarine in a medium-sized mixing container. Use your hands to mix until the mixture is crumbly.
3. Stir milk in with a fork. Mix in cheese.
4. Spoon dough in 1 Tbsp. portions onto the prepared baking tray.
5. Bake at 375° Fahrenheit until golden on top, about 12 minutes.
6. Serve.

# Apple Pancakes

## Ingredients

- 3 Tbsp Unsweetened applesauce
- 1.5 cups almond milk
- 1 tsp Vanilla extract
- 0.25 cups Walnuts
- 2 Tbsp Chia seeds
- 1 Egg
- 2 tsp Cinnamon
- 1 Apple
- 0.5 tsp Apple pie spice
- 3 Tbsp Wheat germ
- 0.5 Tbsp Baking powder
- 1.5 cups Pastry flour - whole grain

## Procedure

1. Prepare a small skillet with a spritz of nonstick spray, and warm it on the medium-temperature setting.
2. Cook the apple with 1 tsp. cinnamon, covered, until tender, about 5 to 10 minutes.
3. Stir together 1 tsp. cinnamon with flour, baking powder, wheat germ, and apple pie spice. Whisk and add in the egg, milk, vanilla extract, and applesauce until thoroughly blended.
4. Spritz a large nonstick pan using a cooking oil baking spray. Heat the pan using the medium temperature setting.
5. Use a cup measure to drop 0.25 cup portions of batter into the pan.
6. You might not be able to cook all the batter at once; that's okay.

7. Sprinkle each portion of pancake batter with the chia seeds and chopped walnuts. Cook until you see bubbles around the edges of the pancakes (2 min.).

8. Turn them over and continue cooking for another two minutes or until done.

9. Top the pancakes with the cooked apples and serve.

# Breakfast Buns

Ingredients

**For the Breakfast Bun**

- 1/2 cup warm water
- 1/4 cup coconut oil
- Bacon dripping
- 3 Tablespoons applesauce
- 1 Teaspoon apple cider vinegar
- 1 cup tapioca flour
- 1/3 cup coconut flour
- 1 egg
- 1/2 teaspoon baking soda
- 1/2 teaspoon ground black pepper
- 1/4 teaspoon sea salt

**For the filling**

- 4 cage-free eggs
- 4 slices nitrate-free bacon
- 1/2 small bell pepper
- 1/2 small onion
- 1/4 teaspoon ground black pepper
- 1/4 teaspoon sea salt

## Procedure

1. Preheat oven to 350 degrees F. Line sheet pan with parchment paper or coat with coconut oil. Heat medium skillet over medium-high heat. Add water to small pot and heat over medium heat.

2. For Filling, peel onion, stem, seed and vein pepper, and chop bacon. Add bacon to hot skillet and sauté until bacon is crisp and almost cooked through. Drain off drippings and set aside.

3. Dice onion and pepper and add to bacon. Sauté about 2 minutes, unto bacon is cooked through and

4. veggies are softened. Add eggs and lightly scrambled, just 30 seconds - 1 minute. Remove from heat and set aside.

5. For Breakfast Bun, sift together tapioca flour, coconut flour, baking soda, salt and pepper in medium bowl. Whisk egg, applesauce and vinegar in small bowl. Whisk in warm water, coconut oil and bacon drippings.

6. Add egg mixture to flour mixture and mix until well combined. Add 1 tablespoon coconut flour or water at a time if needed to form soft and slightly sticky dough.

7. Divide dough into 4 portions and flatten into round disks. Dust your hand or rolling pin with extra tapioca flour to prevent sticking.

8. Scoop loose egg Filling into center of each dough disk and pinch edges of dough together to create round, sealed ball. Place filled buns sealed side down on sheet pan and pat down slightly. Place in oven and bake 20 minutes.

9. Remove from oven and let cool about 5 minutes.

# Morning Glory Muffins

Serves 12 pax

## Ingredients

- 2 tsp Cinnamon
- 0.25 tsp Salt
- 2 cups Whole wheat flour
- 2 tsp Baking soda
- 0.25 cups Pecans
- 3 large Eggs
- 0.33 cups Canola oil
- 0.5 cups Brown sugar
- 1 Apple
- 3 Carrots
- 1 tsp Vanilla extract
- 0.33 cups applesauce
- 0.25 cups Orange juice

## Procedure

1. Warm the oven at 375° Fahrenheit.
2. Mix the brown sugar, oil, eggs, orange juice, applesauce, and vanilla in a large mixing container.
3. In another mixing container, combine the flour, cinnamon, baking soda, and salt.
4. Mix the flour mixture into the egg mixture until thoroughly combined. Stir in the carrots, apples, and pecans.
5. Spoon batter into the muffin tin.
6. Bake until a toothpick inserted in the center of the muffin comes out clean.
7. Let cool and serve.

# Papaya Salad

Serves 4 pax

## Ingredients

- 1 medium papaya
- 5 teaspoons fish sauce
- 1/2 cup green beans
- 1 teaspoon salt
- 2 tomatoes
- 4 cloves of garlic
- 4 cups Sticky rice
- 3 jalapeño peppers
- 2 tablespoons Tamarind Concentrate

## Procedure

1. Put the papaya on a sheet pan and drizzle it with salt. Allow the papaya stand for half an hour.
2. Pour off any juice and then squeeze the fruit with your hands to extract as much fluid as you can.
3. Put the pulp of the papaya in a big food processor. Put in the chilies and pulse for a short period of time to blend.
4. Put in the rest of the Ingredients except the tomato and pulse again until combined.
5. Move the papaya mixture to a serving container and decorate with tomato slices.
6. Serve with sticky rice.

# Chocolate Banana Smoothie

Serves 1 pax

## Ingredients

- 1 Banana
- 0.5 cups vanilla yogurt
- 0.5 cups Skim milk
- 1 tsp chocolate pudding

## Procedure

1. Place each of the fixings for the smoothie in a blender.
2. Work the mixture until it's creamy.
3. Serve and enjoy it immediately.

# Banana-Berry Smoothie

Serves 1 pax

## Ingredients

- 0.5 cups apple juice
- Half Banana
- 0.5 cups Crushed ice
- 0.5 cups vanilla yogurt
- 0.5 cups Blueberries

## Procedure

1. Toss each of the Ingredients in a blender and blend until they are creamy smooth.
2. Serve.

# Morning Frittata

Serves 6 pax

## Ingredients

- 12 Eggs
- 5 oz Feta cheese
- 3 tbsp Olive oil
- 1 Bell peppers
- 16 Cherry tomatoes
- 1 tsp Salt
- 1 Shallots
- 3 oz Spinach

## Procedure

1. This recipe works best when baked at 350° F, so prepare accordingly.
2. Grease a muffin tin with 12 cups. Prepare the vegetables as described in the ingredient list.
3. Using a large bowl, whip the eggs with pepper and salt until frothy. Toss in the vegetables and fold in the crumbled feta cheese.
4. When combined well, divide the egg mixture evenly into the 12 muffin cups, leaving space at the top to let them expand.
5. Place the muffin tin into the oven and allow the frittatas to bake for 20 minutes.

# Oatmeal Smoothie

Serves 1 pax

## Ingredients

- 10 oz raw oats
- 2 bananas
- 1 tbsp Sugar
- 2 tsp Coffee extract
- 3 oz skim milk
- 2 Tbsp Flaxseed

## Procedure

1. Pour everything into your blender, combine well.
2. Serve cold.

# Berry Yogurt Smoothie

Serves 1 pax

## Ingredients

- 15 oz Greek yogurt
- 10 oz Mixed berries
- 3 Tbsp Sweetener of choice
- 1.5 Tbsp Nonfat milk

## Procedure

1. Put everything into a blender and combine well until smooth.
2. Serve cold.

# Cereals with Oatmeal, Egg, and Flaxseed

Serves 2 pax

## Ingredients

- 9 oz Rolled oats
- 2 Eggs
- 5 oz Milk
- 1 Tbsp Flaxseed
- 1 tsp Cinnamon
- 1 Banana

## Procedure

1. Combine all ingredient son the stove at medium-high heat.
2. Cook and frequently stir until you have the consistency you are looking for, roughly 5 minutes.

# Peach and Strawberry Smoothie

Serves 2 pax

## Ingredients

- 0.5 cups strawberries
- 1 cup Almond milk
- 0.5 cups Greek yogurt
- 0.5 cups peaches

## Procedure

1. Toss each of the fixins into a food processor or blender until they are creamy smooth and thickened.
2. Serve it in a couple of chilled glasses.

# Avocado Toast

**Serves 1 pax**

## Ingredients

- 1 tsp Olive or coconut oil
- A quarter Avocado
- 2 slices bread
- 8 tsp Sea salt

## Procedure

1. Spread your preferred oil over your toast and top with avocado slices.

2. Add a bit more oil, and then sprinkle sea salt over your toast.

3. If you want to, you can also mash the avocado slightly and mix it with the oil and salt in a bowl so it can be spread on the toast like butter.

# Cool Sandwich

Serves 12 pax

## Ingredients

- 12 Eggs
- 12 English muffins
- 1.5 tsp Salt
- 1 oz milk
- 12 slices Cheddar or Jack cheese
- 3 oz Spinach

## Procedure

1. Set your oven to 300F and wait for it to heat to the right temperature, and then set a big skillet turned on to moderately high heat.
2. Take a casserole pan and give it a quick spritz of nonstick spray.
3. Taking a big bowl, mix your eggs, milk, and salt until frothy.
4. Rinse off your spinach and wilt it in your skillet. Put the spinach into the egg mixture. Then, put your egg mix into your casserole pan. Bake until eggs begin to set, roughly 15 minutes, then remove from oven.
5. Prepare your English muffins, splitting them in half. Use a knife to cut your egg mixture into 12 pieces. Then, put one piece of egg onto each English muffin, topped with cheese, then the other half of the muffin.
6. Serve fresh, refrigerate for up to 5 days.

# Apple Crisp

Serves 7 pax

## Ingredients

- 0.5 tsp Nutmeg
- 1 tsp Cinnamon
- 5 Red apples
- 1 tsp Vanilla extract
- 2 Tbsp Margarine
- 0.25 cups Brown sugar
- 0.5 cups oats
- 0.25 cups All-purpose flour

## Procedure

1. Warm the oven to reach 375° Fahrenheit.

2. Stir together the oats, brown sugar, flour, margarine, cinnamon, nutmeg, and vanilla extract to create a moist and crumbly mixture.

3. Spread the apples in a 9x13" pan coated with nonstick spray, then top with oat mixture. Bake for 1/2 hour.

4. Let cool and serve.

# Burrito Casserole

## Ingredients

- 1 Green bell pepper
- 2 stalks Green onion
- 1 Tbsp Olive oil
- 1 Portobello mushrooms
- 5 oz potatoes
- 8 oz sausage
- 4 Eggs
- 2 cloves Garlic
- 8 Oz Shredded cheddar cheese

## Procedure

1. Peel and chop your potato into 1/4 inches pieces, setting them aside. Then, chop the bell pepper and mushrooms as well, setting them into a separate bowl.
2. Peel and chop the garlic. Then, add it to the bowl with the pepper and mushrooms. Slice your green onions and add the whites to the mushroom bowl, setting aside the greens as garnish.
3. Cook your sausage in an oven-safe skillet (such as a cast-iron pan). When hot, toss in the sausage, cooking for 4 minutes to crumble. It won't be done. Take the sausage out and put it in a separate bowl.
4. Toss your potatoes into the skillet and cook for 4 minutes, stirring halfway through. Toss in 0.25 c. of water and stir the potatoes, scraping the bottom of the pan and waiting for the water to evaporate.

5. Set your oven to 350 f. Then, add your oil and mushroom mix into the skillet, stirring and cooking for 5 minutes. If the veggies stick to the bottom of your pan, toss in 2 tbsp. of water and stir to scrape the bottom.

6. Crack eggs and add half of the cheese into a separate bowl. Then, return your

7. sausage to your pan and mix well. Pour the egg mixture on top, spreading it evenly across. Top with remaining cheese.

8. Bake for 10 minutes. Then take out of the oven and serve with green onion garnish.

# Cucumber Crackers

**Serves 2 pax**

## Ingredients

- 98 Stuffed green olives
- 4 Sun-dried tomatoes
- 1 cup Hummus
- 1 Tomato
- 8 slices Cucumber
- 4 oz Cheddar cheese
- 2 oz Flaked almond

## Procedure

7. Using cucumber slices as a base, layer cheese and olives on half and cheese, hummus, and tomatoes on the others.

# Cranberry Almond Granola Bars

**Serves 12 pax**

## Ingredients

- 0.5 tsp Cinnamon
- 2 cups granola
- 0.25 cups Chopped almonds
- 3 Large eggs
- 1 tsp Almond extract
- 0.25 cups Sweetened, dried cranberries
- 1 Tbsp Stevia in the Raw

## Procedure

1. Warm the oven at 350°F.

2. Combine the granola, Stevia in the Raw, cranberries, almonds, and cinnamon in one mixing container.

3. In another container whisk the egg and egg white with the almond extract. Dump the egg mix over the granola mixture. Thoroughly stir until incorporated.

4. These protein-rich snacks are sweet with the satisfying crunch of almonds. They make a great energy bar when on the go.

5. Press the mixture into the baking pan. Bake until lightly browned (20 min.).

6. Place them onto a wire rack for five minutes to cool.

7. Place the bars on a cutting surface. Slice them into 12 bars, about 1 oz. each.

# Lemon Berry Chiffon

Serves 6 pax

## Ingredients

- 0.5 cups Splenda
- 3 cups Berries of any kind
- 4 Eggs
- 2 lemons juice

## Procedure

1. In a saucepan, heat the lemon juice and Splenda using the medium temperature setting.
2. Stir until the Splenda has dissolved. Transfer the pan from the burner.
3. Whisk the eggs and slowly pour the lemon juice syrup into the eggs, whisking constantly. Whisk for 1 minute, then pour back into the pan.
4. Heat on medium-low for several minutes, vigorously whisking constantly, until the mixture becomes thickened and light in color, about 2 to 5 minutes. It is done when the mixture coats the back of a spoon.
5. Refrigerate for at least one hour. Place in serving bowls or glasses and top with berries.

# Belgian Waffles

Serves 5 pax

## Ingredients

- 0. 75 cups Blueberries
- 2 Tbsp Canola oil
- 1.67 cups Milk
- 5 tsp Chia seeds
- 5 Tbsp Slivered almonds
- 1 cup Strawberries
- 1 Tbsp Maple syrup
- 1 Tbsp Baking powder
- 1.67 cups Whole grain pastry flour
- 2 Eggs
- 0.25 tsp Salt
- 1 Tbsp Wheat germ

## Procedure

1. Heat your waffle iron.
2. Stir together the flour, wheat germ, baking powder, and salt in a large mixing container.
3. In a separate bowl, beat and combine the eggs, maple syrup, canola oil and milk.
4. Combine the egg mixture with the dry fixings and fold in the blueberries.
5. Spray the hot waffle iron with nonstick spray. Cook a full 0.5 cups of batter for each waffle according to the waffle maker Procedure.
6. In another mixing container, combine the almonds with the strawberries and chia seeds.
7. As soon as the waffles are done, top with the strawberry mixture and serve.

# Baked Avocado and Egg

Serves 2 pax

## Ingredients

- 1 cup Miso butter
- 1 Avocado
- 2 Eggs
- Japanese chili pepper to taste

## Procedure

1.  This dish needs to bake at 425° F, so prepare accordingly.

2.  Take the pitted avocado and scoop out a bit of the flesh. The idea here is that the eggs will back in this cavity, so make sure it is big enough to hold an entire egg. Slice the bottom side of the avocado so that it can sit flat with the wide-cut side facing upwards.

3.  Crack an egg into each avocado half and bake on a greased sheet pan, waiting ten minutes.

4.  Remove from heat, and when serving, drizzle a bit of miso butter on top and sprinkle a bit of Japanese chili pepper.

# Gluten-Free Banana Bread

Serves 16 pax

## Ingredients

- 0.25 cups sugar blend
- 3 Tbsp Ground flax seeds
- 2 cups Gluten-free baking mix
- 2 Tbsp Canola oil
- 4 Very ripe bananas
- 1 tsp Vanilla extract
- 2 Egg whites
- 1 cup buttermilk

## Procedure

1. Set the oven temperature setting at 350°
   Fahrenheit.
2. Mix the bananas, oil, buttermilk, egg whites, vanilla
   and Splenda in a large mixing container.
3. Mix in the gluten-free baking mix and ground flax
   seeds until thoroughly blended.
4. Pour batter in an 8x4" loaf pan coated with
   nonstick spray. Bake for 35 min.

# Cinnamon Apples

Serves 4 pax

## Ingredients

- 1 tsp Vanilla extract
- 0.5 tsp Cinnamon
- 2 apples
- 1 Tbsp Honey
- 3 Tbsp Water
- 1 Tbsp margarine

## Procedure

1. Peel, core, and slice the apples.
2. Heat the margarine in a nonstick skillet using the med-high temperature setting.
3. Add the apples and cook, stirring frequently, for 3 minutes.
4. Stir in the cinnamon, vanilla, water, and honey.
5. Adjust the temperature setting to low and simmer, stirring occasionally, for about 12 minutes.
6. These apples taste like pie filling.

# Thanks

*To all of you who arrived until here.*

*I am glad you accepted my teachings.*
*These have been my personal meals in the past years, so I wished to share them with you.*

*Now you had come to know about Salads and Healthy brunches, let me give you one more tip.*
*This manual takes part of an unmissable cookbooks collection.*
*These salad-based recipes, mixed to all the tastes I met in my worldwide journeys, will give you a complete idea of the possibilities this world offers to us.*
*You have now the opportunity to add hundreds new elements to your cooking skills knowledge.*
*Check out the other books!*